Glacier Park Lodge

CELEBRATING 100 YEARS

PHOTO BY DOUGLASS DYE

by Christine Barnes

Photography by Fred Pflughoft, David Morris, and Douglass Dye

FARCOUNTRY
PRESS

Front cover photo: Wayne Murphy, CPP; www.jmkphotography.com
Back cover photo: David Morris

© 2013 by Farcountry Press
Text © 2013 by Christine Barnes

ISBN 10: 1-56037-561-2
ISBN 13: 978-1-56037-561-6

For more information on our books, write Farcountry Press, P.O. Box 5630,
Helena, MT 59604; call (800) 821-3874; or visit www.farcountrypress.com.

Library of Congress Cataloging-in-Publication Data

Barnes, Christine, 1947-
   Glacier Park Lodge : celebrating 100 years / by Christine Barnes ;
photography by Fred Pflughoft, David Morris, & Douglass Dye.
      p. cm.
   Includes bibliographical references.
   ISBN 978-1-56037-561-6 -- ISBN 1-56037-561-2
1. Glacier Park Lodge. 2. Hotels--Montana--Glacier National Park. 3.
Historic buildings--Montana--Glacier National Park. 4. Glacier National
Park (Mont.)--History. I. Title.
   NA7845.G53B47 2013
   728'.50978652--dc23
                              2013002915
Created, produced, and designed in the United States. Printed in Korea.

17   16   15   14   13   1   2   3   4   5

PHOTO BY DAVID MORRIS

Table of Contents

PHOTO BY DAVID RESTIVO, NATIONAL PARK SERVICE

The Making of Glacier National Park

Louis W. Hill was a young man when he first traveled across the Great Plains and set his sights on the wild and untamed Montana landscape that would become Glacier National Park. He hiked, fished, camped, and reveled in the freedom of the great outdoors.

Of course, Louis was no ordinary boy from an ordinary family. Born in 1872, he was the second son of James J. Hill, founder of the Great Northern Railway, and one of the country's most powerful men. But the sense of awe and wonder he experienced in Montana never left him. It rarely leaves anyone who has taken in the marvels of America's fourth national park.

The power of the landscape is anchored in the ranges of the Rocky Mountains that form the backbone of today's park. These geologic vertebrae began forming 150 million years ago when one tectonic plate thrust over another, rising through the stratified, sediment-filled seabed formed more than 1.6 billion years ago.

Glacier's wildflowers advance up the slopes near Logan Pass as winter snows retreat.
PHOTO BY DOUGLASS DYE

The Shepard Glacier, shown here in 1911, is a small remnant of the huge glacier that once dredged the U-shaped valley below.
COURTESY OF U.S. GEOLOGICAL SURVEY

Three ice ages slowly carved the land, but it was the fine-tuning, most notably the slow grind of alpine glaciation that began just 6,000 years ago, that gives the park's peaks and valleys their distinctive persona.

The resulting panorama created both a physical barrier and an emotional magnet. Early people passed through the land 10,000 years ago, but native tribes east of the mountains saw them primarily as a barricade protecting their bountiful bison hunting territory. The people

The Blackfeet people have lived in this region for thousands of years.

who would become known as the Blackfeet Nation enjoyed a stronghold on their hunting grounds east of the mountains. Tribes west of the divide crossed the mountains annually to hunt buffalo, but such incursions by other people into Blackfeet territory were limited.

The first Euro-Americans, notably surveyors David Thompson and Peter Fidler, explored the region during the late 1700s. In 1803, the United States purchased the Louisiana Territory from France. Captains Meriwether Lewis and William Clark and the Corps of Discovery

began their landmark expedition.
In 1805, Lewis traveled near the
southern reaches of what would
become Glacier National Park.

Still, the mountainous region
saw only a trickle of adventurers,
trappers, and explorers. By the
1830s and 1840s, independent and
fur-company trappers were making
their way into eastern Montana
along the Missouri and Yellowstone rivers.

Plains Indians on a buffalo hunt. MONTANA STATE UNIVERSITY LIBRARY, BILLINGS, IMAGE 1930.59

In 1864, Congress created
Montana Territory, but Euro-American settlement was a long and bloody affair. The land
east of the Continental Divide was claimed by the Blackfeet, as acknowledged in the 1851
Fort Laramie Treaty. Over the next thirty years, however, Blackfeet dominion faded, their
reservation land was whittled away, and decimation of the bison herds led to the starvation
of hundreds of Blackfeet. West of the divide, native tribes were relegated to reservations
based on treaties dating back to 1855.

By the late 1800s, Easterners and conservationists were already entranced by the
landscapes of the West, including Yellowstone, the world's first national park established
in 1872. Still, only a handful of Americans knew about the beauty north of Yellowstone in
Montana Territory.

Work by adventure writers like James Schultz tantalized readers of periodicals like
Forest and Stream. George Bird Grinnell, that magazine's editor and an avid outdoorsman,
read Schultz's piece, "To the Chief Mountain," and, in 1885, promptly made plans to travel
to Glacier for a hunting expedition. That expedition resulted in annual trips and a lifelong

fascination with Glacier country. In addition, his writing exposed the mountainous beauty and wildlife to thousands of others. Grinnell coined the term Crown of the Continent that continues to be one of the park's most famous monikers.

In 1889, Montana became the country's forty-first state. That same year, John Stevens, an engineer for the Great Northern Railway, charted a route over the Continental Divide at Marias Pass, and the railway completed its transcontinental line in 1893. The possibility to open up the glories of Glacier country was real.

In 1895, under pressure from mining interests, the U.S. government acquired a ceded portion of the Blackfeet Reservation for $1.5 million and opened it for mining exploration. Ore deposits proved minuscule, but the unique scenic potential of the region did not. Serious lobbying began in 1907 by Grinnell and others, including the Sierra Club, to establish Glacier National Park. Montana Senator Thomas Carter introduced bills—three

George Grinnell surveys a cirque atop the glacier that bears his name.

times—and all failed. In 1910, Congress finally passed and President William Howard Taft signed a bill creating Glacier National Park. The Great Northern Railway was poised to step in.

Louis Hill had assumed the presidency of the railway in 1907, and while James Hill saw the Great Northern as predominantly a transcontinental freight line, his son embraced the potential of passenger travel, especially to Montana's Glacier National Park. He didn't have to look far to see that passengers were embracing traveling by rail to wilderness locations. His own father was one of the powerhouses involved with the Canadian Pacific Railway's construction of its transcontinental line completed in 1885. The Canadian Pacific was developing tourist destinations in the Canadian Rocky Mountains. Also, the Northern Pacific Railway had created a Loop Tour with transportation and lodging through Yellowstone National Park beginning at its spur line, and the Atchison, Topeka & Santa Fe Railway was staking its claim at the south rim of the Grand Canyon. Louis Hill saw Glacier as a virgin park—a place where he could develop a total tourist project of his own.

With few funds available for tourist development, the first park superintendent, William Logan, and his Washington, D.C. colleagues eagerly accepted the railway's considerable financial contributions. It is estimated that for every dollar the government spent in the early years of the park, the Great Northern spent ten.

What transpired was the largest construction project in any national park. Roads, trails, boats, tent camps, chalets, and lodges were mapped out and constructed. Horse packing trips brought visitors into the park to the railway-built chalets and camps. Hill also arranged for the White Motor Company to provide auto-bus service through the park. Beginning in 1915, those who preferred to stay on the train could see the park from the comfort of open observation cars.

Louis understood many aspects of the business. Prior to becoming company president, Louis had put in his time, working as everything from an office clerk to shop mechanic after his 1893 graduation from Yale. In addition to his business savvy, he was a natural promoter. To let potential travelers know all about Glacier, Hill masterminded a national advertising

campaign that labeled Glacier National Park as America's Alps and implored travelers to forgo Europe and "See America First."

An accomplished amateur painter, Hill hired artists, filmmakers, and photographers to capture the beauty of the region, creating posters, brochures, and paintings. Hill also knew and was interested in all sorts of people. He reveled in meeting guides, rangers, and buckaroos. On those early trips to Montana, he met and became friends with members of the Blackfeet Nation, a relationship that would endure his entire life.

The Great Northern took exhibits on special trains to bring the park to the people. On those trains were members of the Blackfeet Tribe who attended any public event the publicity department could muster up, as diverse as football games and operas. By 1914, the railway's Glacier advertising budget exceeded $300,000 a year.

And Louis Hill had no intention of disappointing passengers once they arrived at Glacier National Park.

Louis Hill established lasting friendships with the Blackfeet, including Wades in the Water (center).

Glacier Park Lodge: Gateway to Glacier

Early guests arrived at Midvale Station on the Great Northern Railway's *Oriental Limited*. What passengers found after their journey west across the Great Plains to the edge of Glacier National Park was a buffer between the expansive yawn of the plains and the jagged teeth of the Rocky Mountains.

Before them, framed by the station's log pergola, was the panorama of the elegantly rustic Glacier Park Hotel set against the majestic mountain horizon. The manicured lawn was dotted with tepees, and the 1,000-foot garden path was banked with specially ordered flowers planted by the hotel's Swiss gardener. Members of the Blackfeet Tribe, hired for a bevy of jobs, greeted guests in full ceremonial garb. Along with the Blackfeet, formally attired drivers and bellmen in polished knee-high boots were on hand to escort guests to the hotel through

Since its earliest days, Glacier Park Lodge served as Great Northern Railway's gateway to the splendors of the park beyond. COURTESY OF GLACIER NATURAL HISTORY ASSOCIATION

13

a Chinese pagoda festooned with cherry blossoms, and into the great hall.

When it opened in June 1913, Glacier Park Hotel (now Glacier Park Lodge) became the Great Northern Railway's Gateway to Glacier, and the start and end point for the railway's park tours. Those tours offered a blend of Wild West "roughing it" that travelers longed for couched in the luxuries they were accustomed to. And that experience began with their hotel stay.

As president of the railway, Louis Hill's first foray into lodging facilities began at Belton, on the west side of the park, with construction of the quaint Belton Chalet near the train station. But his major development unfolded on the east side of the Continental Divide. Both Belton and Glacier Park Lodge properties are outside of the park proper.

Acquiring the land for a hotel in East Glacier and a station at Midvale (now East Glacier Park) was a complicated process, but nothing Louis Hill could not manage. Louis had taken over as

Many visitors arrive in East Glacier by train, as they have for a century. PHOTO BY DAVID MORRIS

The lodge's design reflected an "Americanized-Swiss plan" that the park service later embraced. COURTESY OF GLACIER NATIONAL PARK ARCHIVES

company president from his father, James J. Hill, in 1907, but temporarily stepped down in December 1911 to devote his time to railway-financed projects in and around Glacier National Park. "The work is so important that I am loath to in trust [*sic*] the development to anybody but myself," he explained to the press.

East meets west in the eclectic décor of the lobby. COURTESY OF GLACIER NATIONAL PARK ARCHIVES

Louis Hill's vision for Glacier Park Lodge was based on the Forestry Building (above and facing page), built by the timber industry for the 1905 Lewis & Clark Exposition in Portland. COURTESY OF OREGON HISTORICAL SOCIETY, # BB000442 AND # 26217

Using his political influence, by 1912 Hill had secured a special Act of Congress giving the railway the right to purchase 160 acres on the Blackfeet Indian Reservation just outside the park. The station depot and Glacier Park Hotel would be part of a complex that included Many Glacier Hotel, Lake McDonald Lodge, Belton Chalet, eight chalet camps, and the Prince of Wales Hotel in Glacier's sister park, Waterton Lakes National Park in Canada, along with miles of roads and trails, a telephone system, and motor touring and boat services.

All building construction would mimic the Swiss architectural motif, and the entire

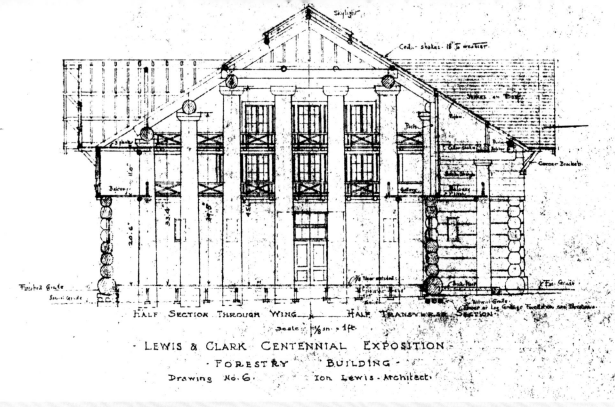

HALF SECTION THROUGH WING   HALF TRANSVERSE SECTION

Scale ⅛ in. = 1 ft.

- LEWIS & CLARK CENTENNIAL EXPOSITION -
· FORESTRY · BUILDING ·
Drawing No. 6.   Ion Lewis · Architect·

So enamored of the Forestry Building was Hill that he had the plans sent to his architect for tracing.

tourist enterprise was based on the European model of mountain destination travel.

The Swiss design Hill admired and executed at Belton Chalet was tempered in keeping with the size and expanse of the East Glacier setting. Instead of Switzerland, he turned to the state of Oregon and its huge timbers to set the tone for his signature hotel.

The 1905 Lewis & Clark Exposition in Portland featured buildings erected by eleven states, but the darling of the expo was the Oregon Forestry Building designed by Portland architect Ion Lewis and his apprentice, Albert E. Doyle. Hill and his father were particularly taken with the structure, which was meant to promote Oregon wood products.

Called the "World's Largest Log Cabin" in the official expo guide, the building featured a colonnade of massive forty-eight-foot-high logs. Three large skylights topped the pitched roof. After the exposition, Hill's father donated money to preserve and maintain the Forestry Building. In 1911, Hill mentioned the donation in correspondence requesting the plans, more than thirty pictures, and the cost of the structure. These materials were sent to his architect, S.L. Bartlett, who then had tracings made of the plans and returned them to Portland.

Over the winter of 1911 and into 1912, Bartlett, with the assistance of Thomas McMahon, created in Glacier Park Hotel a "chalet" with dimensions that reflected America's West.

Since Hill wanted the same impressive colonnade as the Forestry Building, he had the Douglas-fir logs sent by rail from the Pacific Northwest. Specially extended freight cars transported the logs, and when sixty massive timbers arrived, the astounded Blackfeet are said to have dubbed the new building *Oom-Coo-Mush-Taw* or Big Trees Lodge. It's no wonder. Montana might be Big Sky country, but trees of that size were unheard of on this side of the Rockies.

Evensta & Company of Minneapolis was hired to construct the building. By March, Bartlett and the contractor were staking out the hotel and overseeing construction of the workers' camp. Meanwhile, a spur track was being completed to transport the timber now waiting at Whitefish and Essex. By April 1912, all of the oversized timbers were on site and construction began. A core group of seventy-five men labored through the changing seasons, and fifteen months later the lodge was completed.

Built on a slight knoll, the hotel design was long and relatively low slung so as not to obscure the mountain views. The main building features a pitched roofline with long shed dormers, peeled log railings along the balconies and porches, and shingles between the gables. The plan called for log exterior on the main building. After a fuss over pricing, the exterior was covered with clapboard siding and shingles that were more easily procured (and cheaper). The Great Northern hotels first were coated with a creosote stain, but now are painted in what is referred to as national park brown.

For guests, the setting and the hotel's rustic exterior were just the beginning. Stepping through the doors, they entered a remarkable "forest"—indoors. Twenty-four Douglas-firs—each three stories high and four feet wide—line the colonnade of the 200-by-100-foot lobby. Tree bark remains on all of the fifteen- to eighteen-ton vertical timbers, with light filtering through three atrium windows that straddle the sixty-foot-high peak of the roof. Peeled cedar railings inset with St. Andrew's crosses rim the two staggered balconies. Two large, hand-hewn timber stairways lead to the second and third floors.

The image is rustic, but the great hall's rectangular basilica design is derived from that of Roman halls, which was adopted as a building type for early Christian churches. The lobby is a sanctuary of sorts and reflects the idea of architecture as symbol, not just shelter.

The hotel opened on June 15, 1913, but an official grand opening was delayed until June 22 when hundreds of guests enjoyed a free meal at the hotel, toured the grounds, and were entertained by Blackfeet tribal members and an Elks Club band.

The hotel's grand finale that season was the seventy-fifth birthday party of James. J. Hill on September 16. Six hundred invitations went out to the elder Hill's friends and associates, including the railway's engineers, conductors, brakemen, and station agents. Guests arrived in private rail cars for

The great hall features a "forest" of massive Douglas-fir columns, each weighing as much as eighteen tons. PHOTO BY DAVID MORRIS

James J. Hill's birthday guests fill the great hall, served by costumed waitresses. COURTESY OF MINNESOTA HISTORICAL SOCIETY LH 137

the festivities. Following the lavish luncheon celebration featuring mountain trout and Montana beef tenderloin held in the hotel's great hall, each guest toured the park by auto, horseback, or on foot.

Almost as soon as the sixty-one-room hotel was completed, Hill ordered an expansion. A four-story annex, connected by a wide breezeway, added 111 rooms to the hotel. The exterior of the annex features arched brace roofs extending over balconies, supported by

Breezeway windows offer spectacular mountain views.

massive timbers, with jig-sawn balustrades between board railings that add a Swiss touch. The breezeway created one of the most charming additions to the lodge, a departure from the huge, imposing great hall. The breezeway is banked on both sides by windows and topped with the timber beams and trusses of the open ceiling. Filled with Morris chairs, and card tables and desks, it is used today as it was originally intended. Guests read, write letters, play cards, or enjoy the scenery from a sunny, sheltered vantage point.

When the hotel was first proposed it was estimated that it would cost between $100,000 and $200,000. After all was said and done, the cost of construction and furnishing ran about four times the estimate.

Louis Hill was a hands-on manager.

An etched glass mountain goat welcomes guests to the lodge.
PHOTO BY DAVID MORRIS

In addition to the complex negotiations and construction of the park's infrastructure, he kept his thumb on building progress, and he personally selected everything for the décor, from paper lanterns to a mounted eagle his son had shot.

"I want to have the eagle that Louis killed recently mounted. I want him in the Glacier Park Hotel lobby. . . . I wish you would call up Mrs. Hill and get the eagle and have it mounted wherever you think best, instructing them to make a very wide spread of the wings and have the eagle in a flying position," he wrote.

The lodges' back porch frames views of snowcapped peaks.   PHOTO BY DAVID MORRIS

Gift Shop

The Swiss-style lounge of the Empire Bar embraces guests in Old World elegance.
PHOTO BY DAVID MORRIS

Hill's taste seemed as eclectic as his duties. He was an accomplished amateur painter and art collector, architecture buff, booster, adopted member of the Blackfeet Tribe, outdoorsman, and businessman, and Glacier Park Hotel embodied all of this.

While totem poles stood on the front porch, Japanese lanterns hung from the rafters inside. Animal horns and skins, buffalo skulls (some reproduced in plaster of Paris), and tepees, Blackfeet crafts, rugs, blankets, and basketry filled the lobby. Indian pictographs still adorn the walls above picture windows in the lobby, and photographs along with original John Fery paintings were hung throughout the hotel. To emphasize the "camp feel of the forest lobby," as a railway brochure of the time described it, a copper-hooded, open fireplace stood at one end and a more traditional stone fireplace at the other. Immense plate glass windows from six to eight feet wide and five feet high framed the views.

The staff was part of the staging. Besides the Blackfeet Indians, whom Hill often referred to as the "Glacier Park Tribe," kimono-clad waitresses served tea, and many of the male and female staff were outfitted in Bavarian uniforms.

A glass-encased mountain goat is the centerpiece of the expansive lobby. PHOTO BY JASON SAVAGE

Guests fuel their adventures in the park with wonderful meals in the dining hall. PHOTO BY DAVID MORRIS

None of this was a decorating mishap. The international flavor reflected the business interests of the Great Northern. The railway encouraged tourism to Seattle and Alaska, and its premier train was the *Oriental Limited*. The Great Northern also formed the Great Northern Steamship Company to trade with Japan. If the décor with its advertising undercurrent was too confusing, guests could simply walk out onto the expansive veranda running the length of the lodge and gaze at the imposing mountain range artistically composed without the help of man.

Guestroom size and accommodations varied. The second floor featured thirty-six rooms, six with private baths (some with fireplaces), and four public baths to accommodate other guests. The third floor had fewer rooms but all featured interior balconies with views of the great hall and fire pit below. Each room was meticulously furnished, and some original guestroom pieces remain. Glass shades were custom-ordered from Pittsburgh, and rooms were decorated with sturdy oak furniture, Navajo rugs, china candlesticks, and Hudson Bay blankets. A white-enameled, indoor plunge pool filled with heated mountain spring water in the basement was later filled in and the space was used for cabaret shows.

A garden stroll welcomes guests to the lodge's front entrance. PHOTO BY FRED PFLUGHOFT

With its perfect location and accommodations, Glacier Park Lodge drew dignitaries including presidents and princesses. As part of the Blackfeet entertainment, many were inducted into the "Blackfeet White Tribe."

Today, the lanterns and most of the original lobby furniture and accessories are gone. An original half-log table and baby grand piano remain, and a mountain goat (the Great Northern Railway's mascot) is mounted in the center of the lobby. Three oversized chandeliers with Mission-style lanterns and matching sconces light the space. Portions of the hardwood floors are now carpeted. The open fireplace was removed after it caused more than a "camp fire."

The cocktail lounge, once on the balcony, now fills part of the west lobby, with picture windows opening up the entire wall. At one time, the space served as the rest area for the Blackfeet between their evening shows.

The original clinker brick fireplace, with hooks and a simmering shelf, anchors one wall of the dining room. Windsor-style chairs surround the tables. Wagon-wheel chandeliers have replaced at least two other vintages of light fixtures, including the original Japanese lanterns and the milk-glass globes of the 1940s.

Outside, hickory chairs fill the veranda on the west, and flowers still line the garden path at the entry, along with a few tepees.

By the end of 1914, Glacier Park Hotel Company, a subsidiary of the Great Northern Railway, took over ownership and operation of the railway's hotels and camps in the park. Louis

The lodge's swimming pool is a popular guest amenity, uncommon among the lodges associated with our national parks. PHOTO BY FRED PFLUGHOFT

Hill stepped down as president of the Great Northern in 1919, replaced by Ralph Budd, with Hill remaining as chairman of the board.

The company built a nine-hole golf course on additional land purchased to buffer the grand hotel from other development. In addition, an outdoor pool, tennis court, and bowling and putting greens were added—just in time for the stock market crash of 1929 that marked the beginning of the Great Depression. That same year, Louis Hill retired as chairman of the railway he and his father built, and the railway's tie to the park began unraveling. Louis Hill remained a member of the executive committee until his death on April 27, 1948.

The combination of the Great Depression and the switch in travel tastes of the American public from rail car to automobile dramatically changed visitor dynamics. The 1932 creation of Waterton-Glacier International Peace Park brought two countries' national parks together, and boosted tourism during a difficult time. The stunning Going-to-the-Sun Road officially opened in 1933, and is now a National Historic Landmark.

The Glacier hotels, as was the case in most national park hotels, were closed during much of World War II. When they reopened, the task of reorganizing and running the properties fell on Joseph Jeffries of the Great Northern. The summer season of 1946 brought only fifty percent of the usual number of visitors to Glacier Park Hotel. During the 1940s, the railway lost $1,406,298, the greatest portion of that attributed to "outside of the Park at the Glacier Park Hotel," according to a memorandum from the then U.S. Secretary of the Interior.

Although disenchanted, the railway continued operating the hotels, and in 1957 hired an outside manager. The railway spent $3 million renovating and upgrading their hotels, including adding private bathrooms, but the new management removed much of the historic and Blackfeet interior details. In 1960, Don Hummel purchased the properties of Glacier, and formed Glacier Park Inc. In 1981, Glacier Park Lodge, the Prince of Wales Hotel, and other properties inside Glacier National Park were sold to Dial Corporation (now Viad Corpora-

A Red Bus awaits visitors at the front entrance.   PHOTO BY FRED PFLUGHOFT

tion). They are now operated by Glacier Park Incorporated, a subsidiary of Viad.

The sense of place of the classic lodge has changed little over the past century. Details of the eclectic décor were removed over time, but the bones of this grand building stand as strong as they did when Louis Hill built his Gateway to Glacier hotel.

Today, most visitors arrive by car or bus, but Amtrak's *Empire Builder* continues to bring visitors to the park. It takes little imagination to transport oneself back to 1913 here on the edge of Glacier National Park. As a train whistle blows or a party of horseback riders passes by, guests can still quietly rock in one of the hickory chairs and watch the sun fade behind the Crown of the Continent.

The natural serenity of the lodge's environs eases guests into the slower pace of days gone by.
PHOTO BY FRED PFLUGHOFT

Backcountry Building

Glacier Park Lodge has stood for 100 years as the gateway to the park. Beginning in 1910, Louis Hill also commissioned construction of eight Swiss-style backcountry chalets and camps. Originally linked by bridle trails and hiking paths or accessed by boat, most were on the drawing board or opened when Glacier Park Hotel greeted its first guests.

Some of the backcountry locations began as tepee camps, but as the chalet system evolved, tourists could relax after a day of hiking or riding in the comfort of charming shelter and a warm meal in breathtaking settings. Later, tally-ho stagecoaches and then flamboyant Red Buses carried guests to the more easily accessible chalet stops.

The original backcountry chalet camps included Two Medicine (1912), Cut Bank (1913), St. Mary (1913), Going-to-the-Sun (1912), Gunsight (1911), Many Glacier (1913), Granite Park (1913-15), and Sperry (1913-14) chalets. In addition, Belton Chalet (1910), built at the West Glacier train depot, was already accommodating guests who arrived by rail.

Guests venture out from the Belton Chalet aboard an early open tour bus.

Of the chalets, all but Belton, Granite, and Sperry, along with the general store at Two Medicine, are gone. An avalanche destroyed Gunsight Chalets around 1916, and five cabin chalets at Many Glacier Chalets burned in 1936.

Belton Chalet in 1910.   COURTESY OF GLACIER NATIONAL PARK ARCHIVES

The chalets were closed during World War I and II, and most remained shuttered after the Second World War. Car travel replaced pack trips within the park, and the railway's interest was a thing of the past. After growing old and past their usefulness, the chalet communities were dismantled or razed and burned between 1943 and 1952.

Belton Chalet opened June 27, 1910, not as a backcountry stop or a large hotel. The enclave at Belton was a testing ground for Hill's grand vision. Tucked against a hillside near the West Glacier rail station, the original Swiss chalet (now the restaurant) mirrored the taste of Louis Hill and the design expertise of Spokane architect Kirkland Cutter, whose firm did the original rendering.

The three-story chalet, with its gable roof topped with boards and stones, is the most overtly Swiss building in what would become Louis Hill's building spree. The next year the railway constructed two large cabins, Lewis and Clark, and an artist's studio. A twenty-four room "dormitory" (now the main lodge) with a large lobby was finished in 1913. Gardens,

Two Medicine lakeshore, July 1932. COURTESY OF GLACIER NATIONAL PARK

arbors, and a lush lawn buffered the buildings from Montana's wild country.

With the completion of the Great Northern projects on the east side of the park, Belton was all but forgotten. Over the decades, the chalets fell into disrepair. Beginning in 1997, a three-year private restoration project began, and Belton Chalets were not only saved, but also named a National Historic Landmark in May 2000 as part of the Great Northern Railway Buildings.

In 1912, just ten miles from the Glacier Park Station, the tepee camp at Two Medicine began expansion, and by the 1913 season, there were five Swiss chalet-style log buildings, including a two-story dining hall, with total capacity for 146 guests. Soon roads were improved enough to accommodate auto-bus travel, and Two Medicine became the park's most popular side trip.

President Franklin Roosevelt and his family visited in 1934, after driving the newly opened Going-to-the-Sun Road from Belton. That visit sparked a flurry of interest by the American public, but chalet lodging continued to decrease, service flagged, and the Two Medicine complex eventually deteriorated. In 1952, the National Park Service asked that the Great Northern demolish the chalets and leave the dining hall to be used as a general store. Demolition began in September 1955 and by the following May, the last cabins were burned, leaving only the dining hall/camp store. Today, the Two Medicine Store remains a reminder of the once vibrant chalet complex.

The cribs at Granite Park Chalet, which provided lodging, are no longer standing.
COURTESY OF GLACIER NATIONAL HISTORY ASSOCIATION

Sperry and Granite Park chalets fared far better than most. At 6,690 feet, Granite Park is the highest of the chalets, perched on the edge of a subalpine meadow with views of Lake McDonald Valley, the Livingston Range, Heavens Peak, and the Continental Divide. Designed by railway architects, a small dormitory, built in 1913-14, and a larger two-story chalet, constructed in 1914, were completed for the 1915 opening. In 1924, an additional strip of cabins called cribs were built, but these were later dismantled during the 1940s.

As with Granite Park, the setting for Sperry Chalets was magnificent. Located near Sperry Glacier and overlooking Lake McDonald Valley and the Whitefish Range, the railway felt a chalet compound at this destination (at an estimated cost of $11,400) was a reasonable investment. When completed, Sperry cost the Great Northern close to $30,000. During 1912, a crew built the stone kitchen and dining hall near a tent camp that was completed for the 1913 season. That same summer, they worked on the dormitory, and Sperry Chalets opened in 1914.

Both Sperry and Granite Park chalets were sold to the National Park Service in 1954. But

in 1992, these alpine retreats were closed because of safety and environmental concerns. Eventually, it was decided that Sperry and Granite Park chalets would be saved.

Granite Park was restored and in the summer of 1996, returned as a self-service alpine shelter overseen by the National Park Service. Sperry followed suit, but as a full-service chalet that houses guests in one building and serves meals in another. Both chalets are accessed only on horseback or by foot.

In between the "camping" trips, there would be no roughing it at the railway's grand hotels. The hotels have had their ups and downs, but all still stand as much-loved reminders of another era.

Sperry Chalet under construction.
COURTESY OF GLACIER NATIONAL PARK

In the years before construction of Going-to-the-Sun Road, guests arrived at Lake McDonald Lodge by boat, so the front of the hotel faced the lake. COURTESY OF GLACIER NATIONAL PARK

Soon after Glacier Park Hotel opened, work began on Many Glacier Hotel at one of the park's most stunning locations on Swiftcurrent Lake. Many Glacier opened on July 4, 1915. Designed by Thomas McMahon, the 214-room hotel is the largest in the park. A multi-phase restoration that began in 2001 is taking the Many Glacier from an endangered structure to a renovated hotel.

Unlike Glacier's other hotels and chalets, Lake McDonald Lodge was not built by the railway but by businessman John Lewis and his wife, Olive. Designed by Kirtland Cutter, the hotel combines the exterior of a Swiss chalet with the interior of a Montana hunting lodge. Set on the shore of Lake McDonald, the hotel opened June 14, 1914. In 1930, the Great Northern, through a complicated arrangement with the park service, acquired what was then the Lewis Glacier Hotel from Lewis and renamed it Lake McDonald Hotel (now Lodge).

The Great Northern built the Prince of Wales Hotel in Canada's Waterton Lakes National Park; it opened on July 25, 1927. Designed by Thomas McMahon, the

Great Northern spared no expense advertising its Glacier properties, including Many Glacier Hotel shown here. COURTESY OF RAY DJUFF

hotel was the last in the railway's building spree. It is a Canadian National Historic Site.

The three Glacier chalets and Two Medicine Store, together with Many Glacier Hotel and Lake McDonald Lodge, are part of the Great Northern Railway Buildings National Historic Landmark. They are likely the largest collection of Swiss-style buildings in the United States.

Even with what has been lost, the past is very much alive at Glacier National Park.

Glacier National Park: Crown of the Continent

Glacier National Park is an extravaganza of natural riches that preserves over a million acres of northwestern Montana. Created in 1910, the park was named for its abundance of glacier-sculpted horns, cirques, arêtes, and hanging valleys. This majestic landscape is interspersed with native grasslands, forested hillsides, wildflower-strewn meadows, pristine lakes, and alpine tundra.

A century ago, the park contained 150 alpine glaciers. A warming climate has reduced snow accumulation and sped seasonal melting, so that, today, only twenty-five glaciers larger than twenty-five acres remain. Their milky waters tumble off rocks, collect in pools, cascade into waterfalls, and form azure lakes that reflect the peaks around them.

In meadows and stands of trees or along ridges cut in stone roams an impressive array of wildlife. Shaggy mountain goats and bighorn

Wildflowers make the most of a short growing season near Logan Pass.
PHOTO BY DOUGLASS DYE

45

From Logan Pass, the Hidden Lake Overlook trail takes visitors to a spectacular view of Hidden Lake and Bearhat Mountain. PHOTO BY DAVID MORRIS

sheep dot the cliffs, seeming to defy gravity. Cougar, lynx, white-tailed and mule deer, elk, moose, black bear, and an assortment of small mammals such as beaver, muskrat, and mink fill the landscape. Grizzly bears forage for berries and grasses in the valleys and fatten on

Siyeh Creek tumbles out of Glacier's high country. PHOTO BY DAVID MORRIS

insects and ground squirrels on mountain slopes, while two-legged visitors peer through binoculars hoping to catch a glimpse of them from afar. The park is also a birders' paradise, with over 270 species of birds that either live here year-round or visit seasonally. For park travelers, it is an ogler's delight, with one sight to be outdone only by the next. Ever since explorers set their eyes on the landscape, it has been so. No wonder anthropologist and magazine editor George Bird Grinnell called Glacier the Crown of the Continent.

The park is defined by the Rocky Mountains that slice through its protected landscape and cut across the Canadian border into Alberta. Glacier National Park and Waterton Lakes National Park form the world's first International Peace Park, designated in 1932. In addition, both parks are International Biosphere Reserves and in 1995 were recognized as a World Heritage Site.

Glacier celebrated its centennial in 2010. Avalanches, fires, and floods have altered the landscape, and people have filled the roads and trails. Still, nearly all the native animal species present here before Euro-American settlement continue to make their home in the park.

As nature fine-tunes this masterpiece, the pinnacle peaks and plunging valleys of the park will awe visitors for another 100 years.

Mount Gould towers above Grinnell Lake.   PHOTO BY DOUGLASS DYE

Though not from the same angle, these photographs reveal the shrinkage of Grinnell Glacier over the decades. Above, in 1911 the Salamander Glacier tumbles over a rock ledge and joins the Grinnell Glacier below. Below, by 1985 the two glaciers are no longer linked, and bare rock predominates where thick ice once resided. COURTESY OF U.S. GEOLOGICAL SURVEY

RIGHT: A bighorn ram surveys his domain.
BELOW: Hoary marmots live only at high elevations and hibernate nine months of the year. COURTESY OF NATIONAL PARK SERVICE

ABOVE: Steller's jays are year-round residents in Glacier.
LEFT: Two grizzly cubs stay close to mom.
COURTESY OF NATIONAL PARK SERVICE

Lake McDonald mirrors the snowy peaks of Stanton Mountain, Mount Cannon, Mount Brown, the Little Matterhorn, and Edwards Mountain in the park's southwest corner.

A Taste of Glacier Park Lodge

In celebration of the Glacier Park Lodge centennial, executive chef Joe Santangini shares these recipes as served in the Great Northern Dining Room.

Organic Field Green Salad with Sun-Dried Strawberries and Herb Vinaigrette

A perfect blend of spring and summer flavors, this light but zesty salad is easy to prepare and looks as wonderful as it tastes.   Serves 4

Salad
4 endive spears
10 ounces mixed greens
4 handfuls of sweet pea tendrils (sprouts)
8 yellow teardrop tomatoes
8 red teardrop tomatoes
5 ounces (⅔ cup) sun-dried strawberries

Herb Vinaigrette
⅓ cup red wine vinegar
⅓ cup champagne vinegar
½ cup lemon juice
1 tablespoon lemon zest
2 tablesoons honey
1 tablespoon Dijon mustard
⅓ cup shallots, minced
⅓ cup parsley, minced
⅓ cup tarragon, minced
⅓ cup chervil, minced
2 cups grape seed oil
1 cup olive oil
Sea salt
Black pepper

Preparation:
Set out four salad plates. Wash and pat dry the endive spears and place one on each plate. Fill the cup of each endive spear with a handful of mixed greens, then add the sweet pea tendrils, allowing some to drape off the endive onto the plate. Next, slice all of the tomatoes into halves. Place two red and two yellow halves onto each salad. Top with a sprinkling of whole sun-dried strawberries.

To prepare the vinaigrette, add the vinegars, lemon juice, zest, honey, and mustard to a jar with a lid. Cap tightly and shake vigorously until blended. Add the minced herbs and shake again, then slowly add the oil. Season with sea salt and black pepper to taste. Shake once again, then drizzle generously over the salads.

Red Bus at the Weeping Wall.

Pecan Dusted Trout with Swiss Chard, Toasted Barley Pilaf, and Grilled Nectarine Compote

Fresh trout forms the centerpiece of this classic Glacier Park Lodge meal. Matched with a sweet and tangy compote and hearty barley side, this dish is sure to satisfy after a day in the park's fresh alpine air.   Serves 4

Toasted Barley

1 cup barley
2 tablespoons olive oil
1 onion, diced
1 carrot, diced
2 ribs celery, diced
3 cups chicken stock
1 bunch Swiss chard

Grilled Nectarine Compote

6 nectarines
2-3 tablespoons olive oil
1 red bell pepper, diced
1 yellow bell pepper, diced
1 jalapeño chile, minced
½ red onion, minced
2 cups orange juice
½ cup sugar

Trout

1 cup pecan pieces
1 cup breadcrumbs
¼ cup olive oil
4 8-ounce trout fillets

Preparation:

Prepare the barley first, toasting it dry in a sauté pan over medium heat for 10 minutes. Add the olive oil, onion, carrot, and celery and stir; cook an additional 5 minutes. Then add the chicken stock and reduce to a simmer. Cover and let simmer 35 to 45 minutes until the barley is tender. Cool and set aside.

Next, prepare the nectarine compote. Preheat the barbecue grill (or a grilling pan on the stove top). Slice the nectarines in half and remove the pits. Lightly brush the fruit with olive oil. Place the nectarines cut-face down on the grill and cook until lightly browned, about 5 minutes. Remove and set aside to cool. Add the remaining olive oil to a saucepan over medium heat. Stir in the diced bell peppers and minced jalapeño and onion. Then add the orange juice and sugar. While the compote simmers, dice the grilled nectarines and add them to the saucepan. Simmer until the orange juice is reduced by half. Remove from heat.

The trout and chard can cook in separate pans at about the same time. First, begin heating two large saucepans on medium heat, each with 2 tablespoons of olive oil. With a sharp knife, trim the chard leaves from the thick part of the stems. Bunch the leaves and slice into ½-inch-wide strips. Add the chard to one of the saucepans. Next, mix the pecans and breadcrumbs in a shallow bowl. Lightly brush the trout fillets with olive oil and dredge each through the pecans and breadcrumbs, patting to help the mixture stick to the fillets. Gently lay the trout in the other saucepan. Cook for 5 to 6 minutes, and stir the chard while you're keeping an eye on the trout. Then turn the trout and cook on the other side for another 2 minutes. Remove from heat. Place each fillet on a plate and ladle the compote over the trout. Place a scoop of the barley mixture next to the trout and top with the braised chard. Serve promptly. Enjoy!

Montana Sundae

When you think of Glacier National Park, the first things that come to mind may be alpine peaks, mountain goats, and grizzly bears. But once you've tasted this special ice cream sundae, you'll never forget Glacier's smallest—and yummiest—icon, the heavenly huckleberry. Serves 8

Fry Bread
1 pack dry yeast, double acting
½ cup warm water
1 cup warm milk
½ cup olive oil
1 egg, room temperature
¼ cup sugar
1½ teaspoons salt
4 cups flour
1 cup sugar
2 tablespoons cinnamon

Chocolate Sauce
1 cup heavy cream
1 tablespoon unsalted butter
½ pound semisweet chocolate, chopped

Whipped Cream
2 tablespoons sugar
1 cup heavy cream

Ice Cream
½ gallon huckleberry ice cream
2 cups fresh huckleberries (in season)

Preparation:
First, place a metal mixing bowl and metal whisk into the freezer. You'll use this later for the whipped cream.

To make the fry bread, add the yeast to the warm water in a large bowl. Then stir in the warm milk, oil, and egg. In a separate bowl, mix ¼ cup of sugar with the salt and flour. Then add these dry ingredients to the liquid and blend. As the dough forms, work it with your hands into a ball. Set the dough in a lightly oiled bowl, cover, and let rise for 20 minutes. Then punch it down and divide into eight pieces. Flatten into ¼-inch thick rounds and let rest.

Heat 2 inches of oil in a large cast iron skillet to 350 degrees F. Add the dough rounds to the hot oil in batches until they are golden and have puffed up, about 2 minutes per side. Transfer to a paper towel to drain.

In a large bowl, mix the cup of sugar and cinnamon. Add the fry bread and toss to coat with the cinnamon and sugar mix.

Next, make the toppings, starting with the chocolate sauce. Heat the cream and butter in a saucepan over medium heat. Add the chocolate and stir gently until blended. Remove from heat. To make the whipped cream, retrieve the mixing bowl and whisk from the freezer. Add the sugar and heavy cream and whisk just until the cream forms stiff peaks. Serve immediately. (You can store any unused portion in an airtight container for up to 10 hours. When ready to use, whisk for 10 to 15 seconds.)

To serve, fold a piece of fry bread into a bowl and fill with two scoops of ice cream. Sprinkle with fresh huckleberries, then drizzle with the chocolate sauce. Top with a spoonful of whipped cream and dive in!

Avalanche Creek gorge. PHOTO BY DAVID MORRIS

Selected Bibliography

Books and Periodicals

Barnes, Christine, *Great Lodges of the West*, WWWest, Inc. Bend, OR: 1997.

Great Lodges of the National Parks, WWWest, Inc. Bend, OR: 2002.

Buchholtz, C.W. *Man in Glacier*. West Glacier, MT: Glacier Natural History Association, 1976.

Djuff, Ray and Morrison, Chris. *Glacier's Historic Hotels and Chalets: View With a Room*. Helena, MT: Farcountry Press, 2001.

Fraley, John. *A Woman's Way West: In and Around Glacier National Park from 1925 to 1990*. Whitefish, MT: Big Mountain Publishing, 1998.

Guthrie, C.W. *Glacier National Park, The First 100 Years*. Helena, MT: Farcountry Press, 2010.

Hanna, Warren L. *Stars Over Montana, Men Who Made Glacier National Park*. West Glacier, MT: Glacier Natural History Association, 1988.

Hubbard, Freeman. *Encyclopedia of North American Railroading: 150 Years of Railroading in the United States and Canada*. New York: McGraw-Hill, 1981.

Johnson, Patricia Condon. "Artist, Woodman, Booster… the Greatest Press Agent in the Country, Louis W. Hill, Sr." *Encounters* magazine, July/August, 1985.

A brisk breeze snaps Old Glory to attention near the entrance to Glacier Park Lodge.   PHOTO BY DAVID MORRIS

Books and Periodicals *(cont.)*

Kaiser, Harvey H. *Landmarks in the Landscape*. San Francisco: Chronicle Books, 1997.

McCormack, Eileen R. and Young, Biloine W. *The Dutiful Son: Louis W. Hill, Life in the Shadow of the Empire Builder, James J. Hill*. Ramsey County Historical (Minn.) Society, 2010.

McDonald, James. *Granite Park Chalet, Glacier National Park: Historic Preservation Architectural Guide*. Denver: National Park Service, 1985.

Sperry Chalet, Glacier National Park: Historic Preservation Architectural Guide. Denver: National Park Service, 1985.

Moylan, Bridget. *Glacier's Grandest, A Pictorial History of the Hotels and Chalets of Glacier National Park*. Missoula MT: Pictorial Histories Publishing Company, Inc., 1995.

Ober, Michael. J. Robinson. *Enmity & Alliance, Park Service Concession Relations in Glacier National Park, 1892-1911*. Missoula MT: University of Montana, 1973.

Robinson, Donald H. *Through the Years in Glacier National Park*. Location not given: Glacier Natural History Association and National Park Service, 1960.

Tweed, William, Laura E. Soulliere, and Henry G. Law. *National Park Service Rustic Architecture: 1916-1942*. Washington, D.C.: National Park Service, Western Regional Office, 1977.

Park and Public Archives

Glacier National Park Archives and Library, West Glacier, Montana. Architectural drawings Nos. 8175, 8200, 8089, 8175. Correspondence boxes 76, 85, 97. Correspondence files, 1911-16. Glacier Park Hotel Co. Bulletin #4, July 15, 1914. Great Northern Railway promotional brochures. Superintendent's annual and monthly reports, 1911-14.

Minnesota Historical Society, St. Paul, Minnesota. Great Northern Railway, President's File. Great Northern Railway Co. Records: Glacier Park Division, Old Subject Files, Glacier Park Co. and Glacier Park Co., Canadian Div.

Montana State University-Billings Library, Billings, Montana. Image 1930.59, Charles H. Barstow Collection.

Montana State University-Bozeman Library, Bozeman, Montana. Image 33, Collection 10, James Willard Schultz papers.

Oregon Historical Society Research Library, Portland, Oregon. OHS negatives BB000442, OrHi 26217, and OrHi 39112. Photographs: Lewis and Clark Exposition [graphic], Folder 652-D.

Websites

www.cr.nps.gov/history/
www.nps.gov/glac/
libraryphoto.cr.usgs.gov
nrmsc.usgs.gov/research/glacier_retreat.htm
www.nplas.org/index.html

Lake Francis Falls. COURTESY OF NATIONAL PARK SERVICE

Travel Information

Reservations

Hotel reservations for all of the Glacier Park Incorporated properties, including Glacier Park Lodge, are made through www.glacierparkinc.com or phone 406-892-2525 or, from Canada, 403-236-3400. Glacier Park Lodge is open from late May to late September.

Sperry Chalet (www.sperrychalet.com, 1-888-345-2649) is open from early July to early September. Granite Park (www.graniteparkchalet.com, 1-888-345-2649) is open from late June to early September. Belton Chalet (www.beltonchalet.com, 1-888-235-8665) is open year-round).

Directions

Glacier Park Lodge is located in East Glacier Park, Montana, at the junction of U.S. Highway 2 and Montana Highway 49. From U.S. 2, turn and go under the railroad overpass onto MT 49 north. The lodge entrance is on the left. Visitors can also enter the park at West Glacier and take Going-to-the-Sun Road across the park, then connect with U.S. 89 at St. Marys. Drive south on U.S. 89 about 14 miles and turn right on MT 49. Follow MT 49 south to East Glacier Park and the lodge. Directions to the lodge from various start points can be found at www.glacierparkinc.com.

Amtrak

Amtrak services the park at both East Glacier Park and West Glacier (Belton). The Empire Builder stops at these stations only in the summer. Glacier Park Inc. provides a shuttle service at these locations. For more information on train travel, go to www.amtrak.com.

Glacier Park Lodge basks in the late afternoon sun. PHOTO BY FRED PFLUGHOFT

About the Author

Christine Barnes is the author of numerous books on historic lodges in the U.S. and Canadian national parks. *Great Lodges of the National Parks*, *Great Lodges of the National Parks, Volume Two*, and *Great Lodges of the Canadian Rockies* were all companion books to the PBS television series. She was senior consultant and historian for all of the PBS programs. Christine is a two-time winner of the Benjamin Franklin Award for best history book. A former newspaper editor, she is a graduate of Northwestern University. Christine and her husband, Jerry, live in Bend, Oregon.